ॐ

the
DIWAN
of
NAWID

ॐ

Poetry Collections by Mal McKimmie

Poetileptic
(Five Islands Press 2005)

The Brokenness Sonnets I-III & Other Poems
(Five Islands Press 2011)
Winner, Age Poetry Book of the Year, 2012

At the Foot of the Mountain
(Puncher & Wattmann, 2021)

MAL MCKIMMIE

ॐ

the
DIWAN
of
NAWID

ॐ

PUNCHER & WATTMANN

First published in 2024
Published by Puncher and Wattmann
PO Box 279
Waratah NSW 2298

https://www.puncherandwattmann.com
web@puncherandwattmann.com

ISBN   9781922571861

Cover image: Lisa McKimmie
          Green Skip Drawing
          gesso and pigmented ink on upcycled rag paper
          (featured in Rochford Street Review, Issue 38)
Cover design by Robin Phillips and Morgan Arnett
Typesetting by Morgan Arnett
Printed by Lightning Source International

NATIONAL LIBRARY OF AUSTRALIA

A catalogue record for this work is available from the National Library of Australia

Contents

Diwan — Arabic, a collection of poetry
Nawid — Arabic, a male name meaning
'good news', 'glad tidings'

Save me from the lion's mouth
for thou hast heard me from the horns of the unicorns

Psalm 22:21

I sing that the sun is neither
setting in the west nor rising in the east;
that the earth has ceased spinning and
the sun is directly overhead.

You stand underneath it, Nawid,
casting no shadow upon the earth,
free for the duration of this Diwan
(though the desire to transcend Time
can be a greater cage than Time).

But who am I, where am I from,
and why am I singing this?
You do not know and so you
stick your tongue out at me! Right out!

Now you *are* casting a shadow —
your protruding tongued is casting downwards
a thin, inverted, isosceles shadow,
its pointed tip, its arrowhead, piercing your breastbone.

What is hidden there and why does it tremble so?
And what happens now?

When these poems end,
I will sing that the earth resumes its spinning
and so the sun its apparent rising and setting.

Then we will meet again and you will
know who I am and so
make your decision.

Remember Nawid,
when you see me, stick your tongue out!

ॐ

My child, my intimate joy,
I have outwitted and outwaited Time for you,
and here you are.

Now you must begin to forgive yourself your sins,
and the sins of others which you mistook for your own.

Do not ask me to forgive you.
How can one who has never judged forgive?
Forgiveness is a human action
and I have broken open the human.

If you must call my stillness
something that it is not, like *forgiveness*,
perhaps you cannot be here with me.

Are you not here because my stillness called
to its likeness in you?

Listen, Nawid! You must break open the human too.

If once upon a time, many years ago,
my stillness radiated out from the place of my waiting
and found you wherever you were, *when*ever you were,

and broke open your hard and unforgiving heart,
freeing its lament to journey, weeping,
in search of Me,

forget that now.
That was a beginning.
This is an ending.

O how great is the Love of the One who says:

For your sins you will find me within.

What could I say that your ears could hear?
Do you remember?

I once whispered to you the merest secret
and it wounded you almost irrevocably.

Your conception of My nature is not My nature.
Should you with your eyes perceive Me
Then doubt not only what you see, doubt your very eyes.

Whatever you see
will neither be Me nor reveal Me.

Everything that you hear and see and think I am,
I am not.

And everything that I am not
leads to a door that opens inwards like death,
but while you are alive.

I made that door and
behind it I wait for you.

Some people who believe in God
fear that the existence of the God they believe in
is not dependent upon their belief.

They are correct, Nawid, and often know they are.
And so believe and proclaim and proselytize all the more fervently.

Some people who do not believe in God
fear that the non-existence of the God they do not believe in
is not dependent upon their disbelief.

They are correct; they too are absolutely powerless:
this non-existent God would continue to not exist
even if they turned to loud and fervent prayer.
And so they declaim and debunk all the more fervently.

All the while, God goes on existing or not existing
or both simultaneously, as the case may be,

and Creation goes on happily happening
as if God exists in some manner,
even if only — only! — as Creation.

Those ants wandering the rim of the well
are your thoughts, Nawid, looking for crumbs.
They are always hungry. Pay them no mind.

Keep to your discipline. Keep peering into the well,
waiting for God's breath to ripple the mirror until
your face is replaced by another face.

Keep to your discipline even after this,
for God will breathe again and your new face too
will be replaced by another face, and that by yet another.

This will keep happening until there is nothing reflected there
but the night sky's emptiness and a single burning star
that shimmers as both mystery and memory.

O child of the faceless one! O pure sufferer!
You will be a hermit in the desert of your own thirst then,
able to do little but weep morning and evening

slowly filling the well with your tears until
both you and it are brimming over
and you can drink your fill of that star's light.

The God of forms stands resplendent upon
the outstretched tongue of the formless God
and speaks for the formless God who has no tongue

The Father and The Son are one

Be one who is blessed by the Word of God, Nawid,
be one who is purified by and in it,
baptised like the sadhaka in the flow of the holy river

The Father and The Son and The Holy Spirit are one

Hear the Word of God Nawid, and keep on hearing it
in every way possible

Speak the Word of God, Nawid, and keep on speaking it
in every way possible

The Mother and The Daughter and The Holy Spirit are one

The River has nothing to do but flow
and nowhere to go but the Ocean

The Father and The Mother
and The Son and The Daughter
and The Holy Spirit are one

To this place you come,
you who steadfastly refused to forsake or forget your loss,
stubbornly refused to accept the names given it by others,
the beliefs that explained it or explained it away.

Suspecting even yourself, you doubted everything,
and so stripped yourself down to the bone.

Now that you are here you must begin at last to
forsake and forget,
begin to name and explain.

Do you think your loss was yours and so
you cannot give it up?
It was a loan and a lesson.
It was a light though it plunged you in darkness.
It was a life though it almost killed you.

Your unwavering doubt,
your questioning even of your own questions,
your refusals to turn from your own thoughts,
had one purpose and one purpose only:

when first you refused to be filled by others
a hole began to open within you,
an atom at first, invisible;
later, the size of a pinprick,
felt more than seen, like a tremulous fear.

The hole is now the size of, say,
the eyepiece of a microscope or telescope.

If you look through it, Nawid, you will see me seeing you
and so see yourself truly:
how small you are, and how far away from me.
Nothing then will ever be the same.

Be careful, Nawid!

What are your paltry thoughts and imaginings
to the Divine Mother?
She who is both the path to freedom and freedom itself?
What are they to Her?

And how can you dedicate to Her
these beguiling words, ideas, memories and images
that you juggle like brightly coloured balls
if you have become proud of your juggling?

You want to know why it is that
almost invariably in sculptures and paintings
Kali's right foot, rather than Her left,
rests on the chest of Siva?
Who is Nawid to consider Mother Kali's right foot?

If you were to throw straight up into the sky with all your strength
one of these balls you juggle
it would not come anywhere near to reaching
the nail that adorns Her smallest toe.

You are dust that bows to the dust at Her feet.
Your ceaseless thoughts and imaginings
are dust swirling within that dust.

Did She ask you to juggle for Her?
If you were to drop these balls, these trinkets,
these playthings,

your hands and your mind would be empty.
You would have nothing to offer Her but your name.

Offer *Nawid* to Her.

Then offer Her the emptiness that people call by that name.

Six blind men in a room
were trying to identify an elephant.

The six blind men were:
psychiatrist, psychoanalyst, psychotherapist,
psychologist, neurologist and priest.

You, Nawid, were the elephant in the room.

This parable played out for a long, long time:
months, years, decades even.

Then I arrived like a hurricane arrives
and with the violent slap of an open palm
demolished one whole wall of the room.

When the dust cleared you found me to be
a smiling maître d', a welcoming breeze,
ushering you out into the wide, wild night

where you could lumber and trumpet among your own kind.

The six blind men noticed none of this.
No-one had convincingly won the debate
so they kept on arguing.

For all you know, Nawid, they're arguing still,
so far away in in space and time and mind
that you cannot hear them.

I am a hurricane, I am a welcoming breeze,
I am the wind both savage and still,
I am the air that surrounds you, I am the air that you breathe.

Let them go Nawid, forget them.

Even though you are an elephant,
and remember everything.

Yes, of course I call to some of My lovers
from the other side of what they call illness.
I call to My lovers from the other side of
every single thing.

Even sound originating in the same room as you
travels through many filters to reach your ear.
And your ear is the first of many other filters.

All the Nawids you have chosen to be,
and all the Nawids you have chosen not to be,
these are all filters through which My call travels
to the one Nawid you are in truth.

However long it takes. However long.

Yes, some of my lovers suffer from what they call illness.
But some of my lovers suffer from what they call health
and do not even know they are suffering!

It is not My distance from you that is at issue:
I am closer to you than your own blood.
At issue is your distance from me.

Distance, not Illness or Health,
is the true name of suffering.

Yes, I call to some of my lovers from
the other side of what they call illness.

Then, if they answer my call,
I know what their answer is worth!

Did you ever hear of a healthy person who did not die?

They come from another country,
from across the water.

They are strangers, foreigners,
but They live here.

I have always felt a stranger, a foreigner
searching for fellowship,
so I go to Their embassy.

They do have one here, though it takes lifetimes to find,
and I find it, exhausted,
at the very end of myself.

I apply for a visa to Their country.
There is a purgatorial mountain of paperwork
and I have to climb it.

I have to answer every question with complete honesty.
I have to turn myself inside out and upside down.
I must leave no stone unturned and I am heavy with stones.

When I am laid bare both to Them and to myself,
it becomes a matter of Their grace
and therefore my patience.

I must be prepared for rejection.
I must be prepared to continue embracing this place.

This place where I feel imprisoned.
This place with so much beauty that seems so indifferent to me.
This place that I sometimes love so much I feel the love
will kill me.
This place that will one day kill me.

After all, even if They accept me, I will not be leaving.
Nawid will be becoming a dual citizen.

It shouldn't matter to adults
whether they are loved or not;
they shouldn't need the reassurance.

It matters to children.

To adults it should only matter that they *can* love,
because if they can and do
then their loved children

will become loving adults too.

People tell you that they love you
and so convince themselves they do,

as if their love were solely in words and not in
the actions taken and the actions not taken:
the harder choices.

Love itself simply opens its mouth and out comes Time,
out comes Spring, Summer, Autumn and Winter:
Love is the cause behind all effects.

If the human mouth was more limited
and was the only apparatus,
then the words 'I love you' might indeed be enough.

But it isn't, and it isn't, and so they aren't.

You cannot speak even one moment into existence, Nawid!
Not one moment!

You must make the harder choices.

There is a hook in this moment
and in this moment too, and this one and this one and this ...
The moments are different, or seem to be,
but the hook is always the same and always there.

There is a hole in me and it is, moment by moment,
growing in size.
Memories, attachments, faces; plans, dreams, hopes;
things from yesterday and things for tomorrow,
all fall into it, one by one.

Sometimes it seems I am giving them to God,
laying them at God's feet, or, rather,
at the feet of one of his perfected servants.
This giving is accompanied by a great joy.

Sometimes it seems God is taking them from me,
and though this is a greater joy
(that God would stoop to empty the likes of me!)
it is accompanied by a great and wrenching pain.

Every now and then I want to run away,
but God is behind me and before me:

wherever I might run to, there in every moment,
it would be waiting for me — the hook.

One day, one moment, the 'me' in 'there is a hole in me'
will fall down that hole and go the same way as everything else,
as if it were of no more importance.
There will just be the hole left then. And the moment.
And the hook.

I will be empty as a coat, and God will hang me up.
What will happen after that I do not know.
Nawid's eyes have been broken only enough
to see that far and no farther.

People use this expression:
I am at the end of my tether.
I used it myself today.

But a tether is that rope or chain which binds the animal
to a fixed and sturdy post
to prevent it wandering afield, to keep it safe.
(Or to keep it safe for sacrifice).

The Guru is a fixed and sturdy post; the Guru is immovable.
And so I cannot leave, even if I dream of Elsewhere.
I have been Elsewhere, and believe me, it *is* a dream.

What does it matter that at this point in time I do not know
what to do, nor feel that I have the strength to continue?
The rope cannot be broken — it was the Lord that wove
the many threads into one; the Lord that fashioned the knot.

I have travelled through enough illusion to know The Real
when I find it:
I will do what my Guru tells me to do.

Why strain against the rope when the only possible result apart
from exhaustion
is the despair I felt those many years ago
when I was, so to speak, free?

To grieve for one's losses is natural.
To grieve for the losses of others is greater.
To grieve for the loss of one's God is greater still.
To no longer need to grieve? This cannot be measured.

I can no longer wear a rut in the ground
with my relentless circular thinking and thinking and thinking
round and round and round and round:
I am at the end of my tether.

My tether? But the tether is not mine.
Nawid, what a goat you are!

The line that travels to the circumference
belongs to the Centre.

O Lord, take me to my Guru, who is the Centre.
O Guru, take me to my Lord, who is the Centre of Centres.

Keep me safe, Lord.

Keep me safe for sacrifice.

Guru is there

To hold you when you grieve
as Arjuna grieved,

To guide you when you fight
as Arjuna fought,

To guard you while you conquer
as Arjuna conquered.

ॐ

Guru is there

until you and Guru, lover and Beloved, Arjuna and Krishna,
are one and indivisible.

You find this knowledge now in every depth within you
that you plumb.
You see not your own, but your Guru's face
shining in the water at the bottom of the well.

But you cannot help wondering
what is below the water's surface,
behind the mirror,
nor help considering the well itself and even imagining it dry.

Beyond lover and Beloved is the origin of both:
you miss your Guru terribly already.

ॐ

I know, Lord, that none of this means I am worthy of you.

I am a penitent, Lord, and shall ever remain so.

Who is Nawid, Lord, to wipe the dust from his own forehead?

The Lord is putting me in a straightjacket
so that I can move neither left nor right, forward nor backward.
Strap by tightened strap, buckle by buckle,
lock by lock and chain by chain and
throw away the key.

Sometimes, something in me wants to escape.
But it grows smaller and smaller, quieter and quieter every day.
Besides, I am no Houdini.

The Lord knows how desperately I have, in the past,
sought to escape, and all the ways, even the most terrible
(one who hangs his head in shame
may come to hang it in prayer).

But who would want to escape the Lord?
Even when I do not know the Lord
(my forgetful heart is a heart of Blame)
I know my Guru and I know that he loves me.

And I know that he is the Lord's herald and emissary.
He is the Magician's Assistant who ties me in this straightjacket
and having been with the Lord for a long, long time,
knows every trick, every truth behind every illusion.

He knows that the straightjacket itself is my escape.
That one day I will refer to it, without thinking, as merely a jacket.
And so, though still wearing it, will not be bound.

Nawid knows nothing.
He is just an audience member
who happens to have been called up to the stage
and now does not wish to leave.

I look out at the audience and the lights blind me;
I cannot see anybody.
I can barely remember who I came with.
I have no idea how long I've been up here,
for how long this has been happening.

If you were to tell me 'Forever'
I would believe you.

The Lord is naked. Always.
The Lord is a child new to the world, constantly amazed.

The Lord is naked, being alive in the world but dead to it.
What need do the dead have for clothes?

The Lord is born from a human mother. Always.
The Lord then dies and is born from the womb of
the Mother Divine:
this womb is, of course, Creation itself.

The Lord rests in her arms quietly and joyfully and without
question.

The Lord is born in the hearts of disciples:
there and there and there and there ... again and again and again.

The Lord is naked. Always and without exception.
The disciples who find the Lord in their hearts in human raiment,
of any kind, however humble, do not find the Lord.

What is humbler than a nakedness that has no shame?
Humility is a vast silence asking no questions of itself.

The Lord is naked. Always.

If the Lord can be said to wear clothes, then we are those clothes.
We are the impermanent, changeable outer;
the Lord is the impervious, immovable centre.

If we knew this, knew it fully,
Who would we be with the Lord?
Who would we be with each other?
Who would we be in the world?

Tell me please, I need to know.
I can barely stand it.
My whole wardrobe is on fire.

I do not exist in the future, Lord.
I do not exist in the past, Lord.

What I was is not what I am now, Lord.
What I will become is not what I am now, Lord.

Where I do not exist, you exist Lord.
Where you exist, I cannot exist Lord.

It seems the past began when the universe began, Lord.
It seems the future will end when the universe ends, Lord.

But if you have neither beginning nor end, Lord,
there must have been, and must come to be, other universes, Lord.

Other universes or nothing at all. Just you awake, perhaps, Lord.
Then you awake again, Lord, but in a different manner.

All this consciousness! Aren't you tired, Lord?
The past is unfathomably large and the future unfathomably long.

The moment before this moment belongs to the past, Lord.
The moment after this moment belongs to the future, Lord.

This present moment between All past and All future,
this present moment where I exist and so you cannot,

this present moment is getting smaller and smaller, Lord.
I am a pebble being ground between two boulders

of immeasurable circumference.
I am frightened, Lord.

God gave a gift to God.
It was His birthday, Her birthday, God's birthday. It always is.

That gift is not me. I am merely the wrapping.
God is unwrapping God's gift and that is fine by me.
Who is the wrapping to protest?
God is God, and the wrapping,
though necessary because of a mystery,
is still merely the wrapping.

Of course, the fact that God is God
and the gift is for God
does not stop me from protesting, and sometimes loudly.
Unwrapping is painful — at least for the wrapping!

But my Guru comforts me.
He is always there to comfort me:
You'll be fine, don't worry, he says. *What hurts now is momentary.*
That is fine, I tell him, *but what hurts tomorrow is momentary too.*
And he laughs heartily.

God gave a gift to God. But what could it be?
Surely every single created thing,
and even creation itself,
would be, to God, less than a gift.

The only thing it could possibly be is
No-thing, Nothing, Emptiness.

Then, once the gift is unwrapped,
(once I am out of the way)
God can see God clearly, and so be with God.
She can see Him, He can see Her.
They can finally be together.

Nawid can see no other reason for being here.

Nawid! Wake up!
Be vigilant, you idle sloth, and riddle me this:
How many Angels can dance on the head of a pin?

100,000. But only if each is carrying a pin.

And why on Earth would each be carrying a pin?

Because Earth is not all that there is:
On the head of each of those 100,000 pins more Angels dance.

Ha! I like this explanation! But obviously it is not finished.
Can you answer the question I am going to ask next?

On the head of each of those 100,000 pins
10,000 Angels can dance, no more than that (and definitely no less).

No less? Ho, ho! This is getting interesting! Why no less?

Because each of the 10,000 Angels carries a pin
and on the head of each of these 10,000 pins dance 1000 Angels,
and for Angels, numbers are the path to dancing ecstasy.

You are much too sure of yourself, Nawid! Much too sure!
Who are you to say these things about what is and what can and
cannot be?

I didn't say. I am merely reporting the already said,
which includes the 100 Angels that dance on the head
of each pin held by the 1000 dancing Angels.

Already said? By who, pray tell, by who? ... No, wait,
finish answering the riddle first.
There seems to be no end of Angels in the universe!

I presume that if there was a beginning, there is an end.
After all, each of the 100 Angels holds a pin on which 10 Angels dance,
and each of those 10 angels holds a pin on which 1 Angel dances.

And I suppose that this Angel — I am exhausted! — holds a pin?
And I suppose on the head of that pin are more dancing Angels?

Yes, this Angel holds a pin. But no, there are no more Angels.

What then, what? Please finish, Nawid. I am tiring rapidly!

On the head of the pin held by this Angel
sits my Guru smiling his extraordinary smile.

Was it he then, who told you these things?

Of course.

Can you take me to him Nawid, can you? Please?

Get some sleep first.
We'll leave after you wake up.

Don't worry so, Nawid.

The Guru is a whale
that has crossed the ocean

shore to shore, then
has returned for you.

You can be eaten by the loving whale
or devoured by the uncaring world.

There are no other choices.

ॐ

Don't worry so, Nawid.

You have made your choice.
You are in my belly now.

That is why it is so dark.
There is no other reason.

How can I be a householder, Lord
if I don't own a house?

> *No-one owns a house.*
> *You are all renting; you are all passing through.*

If I have no spouse.

> *If I am your Beloved; you have an eternal spouse.*
> *For what else do you wish?*

If I have no children and will never have any.

> *All are children in my eyes and arms.*
> *How can a child parent a child?*

If I have no job, as it is generally understood.

> *This is so you can be in the world but not of it.*

If I am ill so often while others are healthy.

> *What does it matter if you find your illness an obstacle?*
> *Do you think I do?*

But Lord, how can I be a householder if I don't own a house?

> *Sadhana is your house. Your Guru is the landlord and I am the owner.*
> *Live there. Die there. Live.*

People I love see me and say:

Hi Nawid, how are you?
Nawid, my friend, how have you been?
Nice to see you, Nawid.
Nawid, you're looking well! Have you lost weight?
Hey Nawid, how's things?
Brother Nawid! It seems like forever since I've seen you.

And so on.

But I know that when the time comes
God will reach down and pull me up by the tip of my tongue
and so silence me.

How will I then answer those I love
if it means shaking myself free from God's merciful grip?

How will I speak if I am trembling with fear
that I will lose God if I do?

And if I do speak, if through God's grace
I can find a way to do so,
what on earth will I say?
Everything that I want to say?

No.

If what I want to say does not contain God,
God Father or God Mother,
God Both or God Neither,

I will have to let it go.

I might as well begin letting it go now.

I asked my Guru
if he could point out the path to God.

He laughed and stuck his finger in my wound.

You would say it almost killed me;
I would say it killed me.
We would both be telling the truth.

Because Nawid is slow and foolish,
it took him years to shake off
the anger, pain and sadness that overwhelmed him

and realise that his laughing Guru
was merely answering his question.

Merely! He was pointing out the path to God,
the only path to God.

ॐ

I am called Nawid the Forgetful
for a very good reason.
But this? This cannot be forgotten.

To die with one of the names of God on your lips,
this is a great prayer:

  this prayer is a sweet fruit

To live with one of the names of God on your lips,
this is a greater prayer:

  this prayer is a fruit-bearing tree

To die while alive
with one of the names of God on your lips,
this is the greatest prayer:

  this is an orchard full of fruit for others

To die while alive
and become one of the names on God's lips,
this is a prayer beyond great, greater and greatest:

  this is the earth itself

You imagine a God beyond creation
because you were a child once and had a parent and
looking up knew that parent was beyond your imaginings,
outside of you in every possible way,
your First Cause, your Uncreated Creator.

And O the pain of the distance between you!
Creation seemed a prayer torn violently apart
before being uttered, let alone heard.

And so you created a God beyond creation,
beyond the violence, the tearing apart.

You imagine a God beyond creation
because of what you have been taught,
because of childhood hopes, supplicatory prayers,
because of church, temple, synagogue, mosque.
Because of old habits of thought you believe cannot be conquered
without conquering thought itself.

Because of songs and poems,
and the size of Myths that gave birth to songs and poems;
because of inexplicable dreams you've had,
dreams within which you seemed to wake.
Because you once fell so deeply in love
that you could only have fallen from the height of Love itself,
fallen anew into creation.

You imagine a God beyond creation
because you feel broken here, bewildered,
like a stranger who has been told
that the strange house he wanders in belongs to him,
which of course makes both him and the house all the stranger
because he knows that it does not.

You imagine a God beyond creation
because Creation itself
feels shatteringly, unfathomably, painfully, despairingly
alien to you.

But does it not occur to you, Nawid,
that this is exactly how you would feel
if you encountered a God
beyond Creation?

Ma is Mt Kailash and the path up Mt Kailash
and the cave at the mountain's peak
in which Siva sits in perfect asana.

There is no point in asking: *What comes first?*
Siva's meditation or Ma the mountain?
Love does not come before the Beloved,
nor the Beloved before Love.

Both existed prior to Space and Time,
otherwise how could Space and Time exist?

When Siva's eyelids flickered
Ma began to organise the Sky around the mouth of the cave;
when His eyelids opened, She commanded
that a star be born there for Him to see.

When Siva rose from His asana
the whole of humble Space leapt into being at Ma's request
and prostrated itself at His feet.
When He craned His head out of the cave
the wind upon His face was Time.

There is no point asking what we are.
We are a bouquet given by Lover to Beloved.

We are why a smile dawns upon Siva's face,
why Ma becomes a mountain.

ॐ

Do not be surprised, Nawid, if Mt Kailash picks up Her skirts
and tiptoes across continents and oceans as you sleep
to appear as the Mother of mothers
outside your window one morning.
Do not be surprised if you fall asleep in one life and
wake in another.

Just get dressed, put on your climbing boots,
eat a hearty breakfast,
say your goodbyes, and leave.

Ma is just outside the door.
Siva is smiling.

"Listen you foolish little self,
stop weeping at your own misfortunes!

There are people in the world who have no time even to
consider their misfortunes:
they are too busy living them,
too busy weeping for food and drink.
They do not imagine the Abyss, nor
stand at its edge — they are in it.
And their children. And their children's children.

If your Guru gives you the tools to grind wheat
and tells you where to dig for water,
then painstakingly and patiently
teaches your foolish self how to do both,
then you grind wheat and find water.

Come morning, come night,
every day for the rest of your life,
you do what you have been asked to do.
You perform your task with, if not always pleasure, then
always patience.

What does it matter that God does whatever God wills
with the results of your labours?
Do you think anything in God's hands is wasted?

Someone, somewhere, eats.
Someone, somewhere, drinks.

Surely that this daily practice has been requested of you
has appeased forever your own thirst and hunger?"

ॐ

With these words I shake myself, wake myself, saying:
Think thus, Nawid, you fool. Think thus!

I arrive at the Door of the Lord
and am greeted by an attendant Angel
who, with an Angel's curiosity, asks me:
"What is it like to be incarnated
in a human body?"

"It is like entering a town riding a donkey
misbegotten and lame, halting and shabby,
only to find that all the inhabitants speak
(and dream and sing and write)
only and always about horses.

And not just any old horses, never just
any old horses!
But many hands high and brushed to perfection
nimble of step and regal of bearing,
thoroughbreds all, faster than the wind,
mane and tail flowing.

This is the clamour, the pageant,
the captivating vision
that residents enthusiastically describe

while sitting atop
the unattractive and unwanted donkeys
upon which they, too, rode into town.

Unattractive and unwanted because
a donkey that can outrun death is ludicrous.
But a horse?
A rearing, stamping, glistening, muscled,
pure-bred, fantastical horse?
Well, such a horse can try!"

Yes, this is what I will tell the Angel
while Nawid, my ludicrous but sturdy donkey,
who carried me all the long hazardous journey,
sleeps his well-earned tethered sleep.

Many years ago, I left the town in which I was born
out of a foolish loyalty to this stumbling animal
that will be the death of me.

Or not, as the case may be.

Who can see your wound, Nawid,
really see it?
Can you, being the wounded?

You can see it from this side of the mirror.
But your Guru can see it both from this side and the other side,
can see it both open and closed —
can see it healed.

He can even see the unique shape of
the eventual scar.

And your Satguru, the Lord Lahiri, sees it too, of course.
(May blessings rain down upon His holy name!)

Your wound is, after all, the Bethlehem stable
in which your infant perception of His true station is born.

Your wound is the poverty of the Earth hidden
(animals and excrement and dirt and straw and all)
behind the coin and clamor and enticing imagery of the Inn
(you once craved a room at that Inn did you not?)

And Ma sees your wound of course.

She holds all of the above
(and all of the below)
lightly in the palm of Her hand while

laughing with a child's delight
at Her each and every created
and uncreated thing.

If Nawid has another name,
then surely it is Lazarus.

How many times, in this one man's life, the tomb?

To the few close to him he explained
that it was not the dying but the returning
that was the longer and more difficult journey.

Few understood why he wept so when he returned
(those who pitied him would come to know his rage).

No-one knew that he didn't fully return to his body
until the Lord whispered in his ear:
it is not your task on earth that remains unfinished, but you.

For a long time after returning
he woke exhausted every morning
while everyone else bustled about him and into the world.

He couldn't bear noise, crowds, bright lights, reflective surfaces.
For a long time, he just sat and looked at his useless hands.

One morning, after many years of this,
he woke ... happy.
No, not happy, but joyous. Quietly so.

A jar brimming but not brimming over.

Eventually he knew why he had been brought back:
though he was fully alive, there was still something of his death
about him,
like a transparent shroud,
and people sensed it.

And so every time someone turned away from him
he knew exactly why they did so
and could, as a man who remembered dying,
forgive them.

After all, his previous self would have turned away
from this, his new self, too.

This was the gift his master gave him:
there was absolutely no-one he could not now forgive.

Even if it killed him.

If Nawid lays his body, Lord,
at the lotus feet of the Guru
will he receive another body in which to serve you in this life?

If he lays his mind, Lord,
at the lotus feet of the Guru
will he receive another mind with which to serve you in this life?

And if he lays his soul, Lord,
at the lotus feet of the Guru
will his soul be able to one day rise to serve you in this life?

I hardly know what I mean, Lord.
However strong the light
under which I write these words
I write them in the dark.

Nawid hardly knows ...
Rather, Nawid *does not* know
the mysteries of body and mind, Lord.
And yet he has the temerity to mention the soul!

Whatever body and mind and especially soul are, Lord,
together they make your servant Nawid,
and with them he loves you,
knowing that you are the origin of his happiness.

Whatever body and mind and especially soul are, Lord,
together they make your servant Nawid,
and with them he fears you,
knowing that you are the destination of his weeping.

Have mercy on your son, Nawid,
as he writes the words *body* and *mind* and *soul*
though he knows not their meaning,
though he writes them in the dark that he is in.

Have mercy on him, Lord.

Loving him is freeing him
from every human heaviness I would place in his arms
rather than carry myself,

from everything I would burden him with
rather than be burdened with myself.

Loving him is freeing him,
moment by moment,
from everything I hope of him, every expectation I have,

from all my imaginings, every untrue projection.
And *every* projection is untrue.

My image of him is not him.

Loving him is freeing him
from my wants and needs,
from everything that does not spring as pure
as a love freed from wants and needs,

from everything in this disciple
that is not worthy of a Guru's love
(and from my misconceptions about what is and what is not
worthy of a Guru's love).

In other words,
if Nawid is to truly love his Guru,
he must free his Guru from Nawid.

Why fear sudden imbalance, Nawid?
If you let go of your heavy past

the scales that your Guru holds
will not even shudder:

the weight of the past in his left hand
is exactly equal to the weight of the future in his right.

Between the past and the future,
between his left hand and his right — his Heart.

Drop the past, and you will drop the future.
Drop the past and the future, and you will weigh nothing.

You will float as a feather in the present moment,
float upwards in your Guru's Heart.

You are most necessary, Nawid, most necessary.
You are a feather missing from one of God's immeasurable wings.

It awaits your perfect, weightless return.

Do not be afraid.
At the centre of this mystery, Nawid,

is not your need for God,
but God's need for you.

You could say it is a simple syllable, Nawid,
one of myriad possible sounds,
but it is one of the faces of the triune God,
and the only face not veiled by another:
to human beings it is the closest.

Why would you ignore it?

It is not only one of the faces of the triune God,
it is, itself, triune:
like a river and the banks it flows between.

I have sent you a Guru, Nawid.

He may seem like a sober man
when viewed from without,
but when viewed from within
(where *I* am)
he is staggeringly drunk.

He didn't fall in the river by accident — he dived in eagerly!
Such was his faith.

I lifted him into a new life on the opposite bank,
taught him how to swim the river,
and then sent him back.

Now he walks among you quietly without a drop on him.
But know that within him the river roars and flows.

I have sent you a Guru, Nawid.
He may not be Me
but I am him.

Act accordingly.

The Sun is rising as a woman,
She is tugging at the sea-foam in my beard
waking me from a dark night long and stubborn.

She is nudging the horizon with a struck match,
She is showing me the pink of Her tongue and laughing
with a mischief that sets the world on fire,
that turns my heart upside-down —
Upside-down, she says, is the heart's right side up!

She is lighting the Earth leaf by leaf, stone by stone,
as if placing candles one by one upon a cake.
Now she is handing me a present cupped in Her hands and so
wrapped in the Cosmos itself, in manifold Creation.
The present she is handing me is Sushumna, the one path,
the Nothing that leads to the centre of Everything.

Everybody must have been mistaken, all those years ago:
this, surely, is my birthday!

What does my long nightmare matter now?
Everything flows from Her pointed finger, Her decree.

I loved Her — or I tried to, desperately — even while in darkness,
when She was formless, hidden, when She didn't have a name.

Now, finally, She is rising as the Sun and I have no idea why.
Yesterday may as well have not even happened
and I know nothing about tomorrow.

Don't ask Nawid why, I have no idea why,
I don't know a single thing!

Jai Ma! Jai Ma! Jai Ma Anandamayi!

Nawid's grief is like Arjuna's:
it cannot be measured, nor can it be known.

Not by you.

Can you know the thoughts and feelings of a corpse
as it walks among you, the oblivious living,
seemingly one of you, but overcome,
overcome completely.

By what?

By his Krishna,
his consoler, comforter, charioteer,
the Friend of friends who equips, trains, readies him for
a necessary war;
then steers him toward and through it,
holding and healing Nawid the warrior
as he seems (to you)
to lay waste to himself.

You worry about him — but he is no longer one of you.
Your helping hands are grasping hands — they hold him back.
Your words, always the same words — exhaust him.

Let him go now.
Let him let go.
Let go.

Nawid's happiness cannot be measured,
nor can it be known.

Not by you.

Nawid rose, exhausted,
heavy with water, wet as a rat.
He felt half alive, or less than half.

Nawid rose where he found himself,
on the shore at the mouth of the river
after what seemed many lives of desperate swimming
fighting currents and eddies, riptides and rapids,
fighting to stay afloat and undistracted,
fighting even his own dark longing for the darkness beneath him,

and this while trying
to love the roaring river, love it utterly,
with a full embrace and without condition,
even if it should kill him.

And it must be said that at the same time
he had to evade the clutches of those
who would cry out from the riverbanks *Nawid!*
and point, and run, gather others and equipment,
wave their arms, shout unintelligible words,
try to 'rescue' him.

All this because Nawid, like the river, longed for the ocean.

ॐ

Nawid rose, exhausted,
and his rising took, it seemed,
months, perhaps years,

but when he was finally standing upright and dry
there, before him, was a Friend of God,
smiling and assuring him that all would be well,
for now there was just an Ocean to cross.

Just an Ocean!

And Nawid, who was exhausted,
having barely survived the river,
could not be happier.

This is what Nawid believes:

Jesus didn't sacrifice Himself,
He was murdered.

For those in their right minds
the manner of His dying
became a symbol and a lesson

and they shouldered their own crosses
and climbed the Hill of the Skull,
which is just to say

they embraced Reality
and not the world that shuns it.

To put it another way:

It is not His blood that cleanses us
but the full acceptance of our own blood
running through our veins,
running all the way to one day running out.

And, later, the acceptance that
this blood is not ours,
but God the Father's and God the Mother's
and that we are all God's children,
every single bleeding one of us.

To put it yet another way:

He had conquered Himself, His self,
long before the cross,
and so what mattered to Him was the manner of his dying
and not the fact itself.

For us,
the beneficiaries of the symbol, the lesson:

the first nail skewered *I*
the next nail *Me*
the long nail through both feet
pierced *My* and *Mine*

and the lance in the side marked the end
of all of them at once,
so that when He rose, He rose saying:

You, You, You, You, You.

But this was what he was saying as he died,
and before he died,
and when he was walking around in the world unhindered.

So the cross is a symbol, a lesson.

ॐ

All Nawid really knows is
something happened that day,
something that rent the sky,
tore a hole in Time,
made the wind howl for darkness
in the middle of the day.

Something that should have brought down
every church before it was built.
Something that brings Nawid to his knees.

Even though he doesn't believe,
even though he knows that while there may have been
one Jesus of Nazareth
there have been, is, and will be, many Christs,
both male and female.

So even if he calls Jesus Lord, and he does,
he calls another Lord too, and another, and another ... and so on.

Nawid may as well spend the rest of his life on his knees.

Lord, it is Nawid again!
I stand here in darkness, Lord,
before a closed door that I cannot see.

I know that I cannot prove the existence of the door.
I cannot even prove that it is closed.

I know that because it is dark
my eyes may be shut. I may even be blind.

I concede that I have been wrong about light. Very wrong.
Why could I not be wrong about this darkness and its cause?

I concede that my eyes may be closed,
though I do not think they are;
that I may be blind,
though I do not think I am.
I have been wrong about too much, Lord,
to begin to believe I am now right.

And what does it matter if it is dark, or why?
The Sun knows the darkness like the back of its hand:
the darkness *is* the back of its hand.

And what does it matter if I *am* blind?
There is more than one kind of blindness,
and my skin, my whole body,
has eyes to see the Sun.

What matters is the door. That it is there. Or seems to be.
That it seems, at the moment, closed.

O but I concede, Lord, yes, I concede,
that it is I who may be closed,
closed to such a door being open, even *always* open,
to the likes of me,

and that therefore all that can be truthfully said is
the way Nawid feels about Nawid
is like darkness and a closed door.

ॐ

O Lord, it is Nawid again!
And I am standing here,
in darkness or in light,

possibly seeing, possibly blind,
standing before a door that, if it exists,
is either open or closed.

I am utterly bewildered, Lord.
I do not know who or what I am,
nor who or what I am not.

But still I, a dishevelled and lopsided servant
whom God, in His infinite Mercy,
has stripped of worldly name,

I, an obstinate and quarrelsome servant
whom the Goddess, in Her infinite Wisdom,
has renamed Nawid,

I stand here, Lord.

Waiting.

Nawid arrived at his Guru's feet
atop a wild and restless stallion that was
many hands high but thin and ungroomed and
covered in scratches and wounds;
at the look in its eye, people took a step or two back and tensed.

Riding side-saddle behind Nawid, one arm around his waist,
was a beautiful woman, her face turned away
from all that was oncoming;
whether this was because of fear, disdain, modesty or shyness
was impossible to tell.

Sitting crouched on Nawid's shoulders,
fiercely clutching at Nawid's ears to keep his balance,
was a small, unkempt and ragged man, muttering to himself;
he was obviously one of the poor, he was quite possibly mad.

In front of Nawid, but facing backwards,
its arms around Nawid's neck and hanging on for dear life,
bouncing and swinging with the horse's unpredictable progress
was a small child overwhelmed by fear,
eyes screwed tightly shut.

On the crown of Nawid's head stood a clamorous bird,
pecking and scratching, scratching and squawking while flapping
its wings,
one of which was injured and awry;
its beak was sharp and blood ran freely down Nawid's face.

Thus apparelled, thus accompanied, thus encumbered,
Nawid arrived and told the man who would become
his Guru
that he had wandered far, on foot, and alone.

That he had left everything behind.

That he was ready.

ॐ

The darkness that you wandered in for a long, long time

By the Grace of God

The saving light and warmth of the fire that you found

By the Grace of God

The wind that blew over the sea, bearing voices from another shore

By the Grace of God

The spark that leapt from the fire onto that wind, and so into
your mouth

By the Grace of God

The new fire that spark ignited, raging for years, burning your
tongue to its root

By the Grace of God

The wind untrammelled then, moving into and out of your mouth
as it pleased

By the Grace of God

The Diwan of Nawid

By the Grace of God

Notes

Pages 60/61:
Who can see your wound, Nawid,

And your Satguru, the Lord Lahiri, sees it too, of course.

Sri Sri Yogiraj Lahiri Mahasaya,
The Polestar of Kriya Yoga,
30th September 1828 – 26th September 1895.

Pages 70/71:
The Sun is rising as a woman,

Jai Ma! Jai Ma! Jai Ma Anandamayi!

Sri Sri Ma Anandamayi (or Anandamayi Ma),
'The Blissful Moher' and 'The Flower of India',
30th April 1896 – 27th August 1982.

Acknowledgements

The Diwan of Nawid was written on unceded land traditionally owned by the Wurundjeri Woi Wurrung people. The author pays his respect to Elders past, present and future, and to all Aboriginal and Torres Strait Islander peoples.

I thank my sister, the artist Lisa McKimmie, for the cover image, and Linda Adair and Mark Roberts for featuring Lisa and her art and some poems from my next book in *Rochford Street Review, Issue 38.* My gratitude to the ever-supportive David Musgrave of P&W, and to Ross Gillet and Morgan Arnett. I am indebted to friends and colleagues who have read this manuscript or parts of it, including Judith Beveridge, Toby Davidson, Tina Giannoukos, Priya Kaul, Jennifer Harrison, Kevin Hart, Mark Reid and Philip Salom. And my love and gratitude as always to Lynette Satalich, to whom I owe more than I can say.

www.ingramcontent.com/pod-product-compliance
Lightning Source LLC
Chambersburg PA
CBHW031003090426
42737CB00008B/656

9 781922 571861